I Made Some Brownies
and they were pretty good

Other books by Jim

I Went to College and it was okay
I Got a Job and it wasn't that bad

I Made Some Brownies
and they were pretty good

by Jim

Andrews and McMeel
A Universal Press Syndicate Company
Kansas City

I got up pretty early this morning.

While I opened Mr. Peterson's food, she walked back and forth, rubbing up against my legs, meowing.

meow *meow*

Sometimes she wouldn't so much rub as slam the side of her body into my leg.

meow

I worked at the copy store from 9 to noon.

Today I went to visit Ruth.

We walked around by where she lives.

We saw some kids playing in a playground.

And a big truck.

Today when I came home my clock was flashing 12:00.

I figured there was probably a power outage or something

So I reset it.

A guy came into the copy store today and told me he forgot his original in our copy machine.

I looked in the lost-n-found box and couldn't find it.

I told him that people lose their originals there all the time.

But his was important, he said.

Steve called me today just to see what I was doing.

I said I wasn't doing much of anything.

"Well, maybe we could get together and do something," he said.

We came up with a lot of ideas for what we could do, but neither of us felt like doing any of them.

Today Steve came over and said, "Happy birthday, Jim," and handed me a present.

I told him my birthday was yesterday and he said, "Yeah, well, here's a present anyway."

crackle

crumple rip

It was an address book.

Today I decided to write down some addresses of people in my new address book.

I wrote down my mom's, dad's, grandma's...

Then Tony's, Ruth's, Steve's...

I suddenly realized that I hardly know anybody at all.

Today Steve, Ruth and I were sitting around talking about bugs, among other things.

Ruth said, "There's nothing worse than having a mosquito buzzing around your ear."

"Except having your knee caps sawed off maybe," Steve said.

"That's awful," Ruth said. "How could you even think of such a thing?"

Today Tony came by and said he played pool the other day. "It was great," he said.

He asked me if I wanted to play pool with him.

I said sure, why not.

While we played, Tony licked his lip and concentrated really hard when he shot.

I played pool with Tony again today.

Whenever he would make a shot, he'd say, "Alright! That was somethin', eh, Jim?"

But when he'd miss several shots in a row, he'd say, "Geez, what's wrong with me? This is ridiculous!"

While we were walking out of the pool hall, he said, "Pool is just the coolest sport, isn't it?"

I said I thought it was okay.

Today I was pouring myself a glass of water.

Mr. Peterson was standing behind me, looking at me.

She looked like she was just curious about what I was doing, so I showed her the water.

Today I noticed my clock was flashing 12:00 again.

I checked to see if it was fully plugged in.

It was.

I couldn't figure out what was the matter with it.

Ruth moved out of her apartment today, and I helped her.

She had all her stuff packed into boxes and ready to go.

She kept mentioning her sofa and how she was worried about how we would get it to fit through the door.

But when the time came to take it away, it was no problem at all.

I went over to help Ruth again today.

She was in her new place but wanted help unpacking things.

She had all the boxes sorted in each respective room.

But before we did any work, she made lemonade and we sat and relaxed.

I was just lying in bed today when I started getting really sleepy.	I half-fell asleep, thinking about boxes being packed, and having little dreams where I had to make sure everything was packed right.	I woke up when a car horn honked continuously for about two minutes right outside my window. Honk	I got out of bed and was so dazed I could barely walk without falling.
Today I was eating a cheese sandwich when I noticed my clock was completely blank.	Then, after a minute, it started to flash 12:00 for a while, then it went off again.	I went over to see what was going on.	I saw Mr. Peterson wrestling with the cord, making it move slightly in and out of the socket.

Tony came by today.

I thought he'd want to play pool, but he said, "Ah, I'm sick of pool."

We ended up watching the news on TV.

Tony pointed at the newscaster and said, "Get a loada that guy's hair!"

Today I bought a rotating thing for the microwave that runs on batteries.

I heated up some beans and watched them turn around slowly on the rotating thing.

They started bubbling after a few seconds.

After they were done and the oven turned off, I kept watching them turn around for a while.

I came home from the copy store today, made a peanut butter sandwich, and watched TV.

When I was done eating I felt really tired.

After a while, I realized I wasn't paying attention to the TV, but I didn't have enough energy to turn it off.

At the copy store today we got a shipment of paper.

I helped unload it from the truck.

Julie was standing by the back door, where we were stacking the boxes.

"Oh good," she said, "more paper."

I went walking around today.

I walked by a big corporate headquarters of a bank or something.

They had patches of grass and some potted trees in a big cement area by the main entrance.

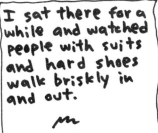

I sat there for a while and watched people with suits and hard shoes walk briskly in and out.

Today Tony drove me around because he had his brother's car for the day.

"we'll go cruisin' for chicks!" he said.

We stopped at a red light and Tony tapped his hands on the wheel.

We sat there a long time and Tony yelled, "come on—change!" and then the light finally changed.

I was trying to open my window today to get a little breeze.

But it wouldn't stay open by itself.

So I put a book under it to hold it open.

Then Mr. Peterson and I sat there and just looked out the window for a while.

I went to a gift shop with Ruth today.

She bought a calendar with pictures of puppies and kittens on it.

"They're so cute," she said. "I just love 'em!"

She told me she almost got the "Rear View" calendar.

Tony came by today to tell me he had a girl-friend.

"I really think this is it, Jim. I think I'm in love," he said.

I asked him what her name was and he said, "Jaime—I mean Jill. It's Jill."

He realized how funny it was to stumble on the word. "Yeah, duh— I can't even say her name," he said

Tony brought his new girlfriend, Jill, over today.

"Jill, I just wanted you to meet my buddy, Jim," he said.

We said hi to each other.

After a few seconds, Tony said, "I just wanted you two to meet."

Today Ruth and I ate at a pancake restaurant.	While we were waiting for our food, we read the paper place mats.	On the backs they had games and puzzles for kids to play.	Ruth wanted to play the dot-to-dot but neither of us had a pen.

I let Mr. Peterson outside for a little while today.	Like usual, she was really scared, and stayed pretty much in one place.	But she eventually explored all the stairs near the door.	After she did that, she went back to her space and stayed there.

Today I went out on a bike ride.

I stopped by a ball park and watched part of a little league game or something.

I liked the way the sound of the bat hitting the ball echoed across the park.

It was almost dark by the time I got back home.

I saw Tony today on the way to my mailbox.

He was with his new girlfriend, Jill.

They both said "Hi, Jim," in unison as they passed me.

I got my mail and all I got was a flyer about a missing child.

Have you seen Doug?

I got a newspaper today and sat at the table to read it.

Mr. Peterson jumped up on the table and stood on the newspaper.

I put her back on the floor.

Then she ran into the other room and meowed over and over.

meow meow

Today Ruth and I went driving around.

She was running a bunch of errands and I just came along.

We went to a couple of stores, the post office, and places like that.

Post Office

When we were done, Ruth said. "That was kind of fun, wasn't it?"

I decided to start reading a book today.

It's I, Robot, by Isaac Asimov. (Steve told me it was a pretty good book and I should read it.)

when I sat down to read, Mr. Peterson was sitting on the table, just across the room from me.

Every time I would try to start reading, Mr. Peterson would look at the ceiling and meow, and I couldn't concentrate.

I read some more of my book today.

(It's I, Robot.)

So far, I think it's a pretty good book.

Today I had to clean my kitchen.

I scrubbed out the sink, mopped the floor, and everything

Mr. Peterson watched, but was too scared to get any closer than a couple of yards away.

After I was done, she cautiously stepped into the kitchen, sniffing the floor and the air.

I was woken up today by the phone ringing.

Ring

It was somebody I didn't recognize saying, "Al—you slept in, huh, ace?"

After that, I tried to get back to sleep, but couldn't.

Mr. Peterson was scratching the wall, something was tapping on the ceiling—every little noise seemed extra loud.

I finished reading I, Robot today.

It was a short book, so it didn't take me very long to read it.

Steve, who was the one who told me I should read it, said, "How'd you like it?"

I said I thought it was a pretty good book.

Today I felt like eating a fried egg.

It'd been so long since I had a fried egg that for a second I couldn't think of how to make one.

But it was only for a second.

Once I realized I knew how to do it, I knew it was really easy.

I saw Tony and Jill again Today.	They both said hi to me as I passed them.	Later in the day Tony stopped by.	"Jim," he said, "you ever know somebody who did little things that just <u>bugged</u> you?"

I saw Tony Today. He had just come back from picking up his mail.	I asked him where Jill was.	"You don't wanna know," he said.	He flipped through his mail to see what he got.

At the copy store today I worked with Hal.	While he was looking at the copy we made, I noticed how tightly curled his hair is.	He showed me some paste-up marks he found on the copy, and told me to touch them up.	"This wouldn't happen if we had one of those Canon 6650's," he said.

I was walking outside today when I noticed a squirrel by a tree.	He looked at me, then ran up the tree.	Then I came home and saw Mr. Peterson.	She dashed out the door as soon as I opened it.

I walked past my chair today and noticed Mr. Peterson chewing on it.

When she saw me she ran away.

I sat down to watch some TV.

Nothing was on.

Today Tony told me he had decided to get a better job.

(For the past few months he's been working at the shoe store where his brother's the manager.)

"There's no future in shoes," he said.

He asked if I'd help him write a résumé and I said I would.

I made myself a peanut butter and jelly sandwich today and sat down to eat it.

I thought I'd listen to the radio while I ate.

I tuned in a few stations to find something good.

But nothing good was on.

I helped Tony with his résumé today.

We sat around and tried to make his job experiences sound really good.

He was getting frustrated because he's only worked at a grocery store, an ice rink and the shoe store.

"These jobs make me sound like just some boob who's never accomplished anything!" he said.

I helped Tony work on his résumé again today.

Tony said we should work on sharpening up the fine points.

(He was eating a Hostess pie.)

"Like this," he said. "Instead of 'worked' at ice rink, say 'organized' or 'managed.'"

He also said that when he takes it to the printer, he'll pick out a type style that will fix up the whole thing.

I got up early today and was really tired.

I fed Mr. Peterson, took a shower, and ate some cereal...

But even then I was still really tired.

So I slept for a little while longer.

I was walking home from work today when I realized I forgot my coat.

It was a pretty nice day outside, and I didn't really need a coat.

But I went back to the copy store to pick it up anyway.

Julie was there, and didn't even notice that I'd come back.

There was somebody new at the copy store today.

Hal said, "Dan just started today—will you show him how to work the big copier?"

I showed him what all the buttons and dials did, and how to set them.

I explained how to enlarge, reduce, collate, change trays, and everything.

Dan was working at the copy store again today.	He was having trouble making a copy, so I showed him how to do it again.	"Oh, yeah, of course. I forgot that part," he said.	I felt really tired that night, and fell asleep really early.

Today I was tired, so I fell down onto my bed.	I thought I might fall asleep.	But Mr. Peterson walked onto my back and started kneading me with her paws.	Her claws were sharp and there was no way I could fall asleep with her doing that.

Today I made a peanut butter and jelly sandwich and sat down to eat it.

I put a lot of jelly on it and it started oozing onto the plate.

I turned the sandwich over so the big clumps of jelly would be on top.

But then it started to ooze out the bottom.

I slept in late today and felt really tired.

I probably got too much sleep.

I had my lunch break with Dan today.

He told me there were seven kids in his family, and he was number five.

I slept in late again today.

I just really felt like sleeping.

Normally that feeling wears off during the day.

But today I felt tired all day.

I got out my big winter coat today.

After I put it on I found a dollar bill in the pocket.

I didn't remember putting it there last winter, so it was kind of a nice little surprise.

I ran into Tony and he said, "The world might as well end right now, Jim."

Today I was talking to Tony.	He was telling me all about the hard time he was having finding a job.	"I sent all my résumés out, but nobody's calling!" he said.	He told me he doesn't think he can stand his brother's shoe store for one more day.

Today at the copy store, Joel was showing Dan how to fill the copier with toner.	He explained it kind of quickly and then told Dan to try it.	Dan didn't do it right and Joel said, "c'mon, it's simple," and explained it again.	"I can't teach this guy anything," he said.

Today I noticed Mr. Peterson batting something around on the floor, so I picked it up.

She backed up and got ready to pounce, as if waiting for me to throw it back to her.

I looked closely at it and it was a thin blue plastic thing with a little ridge on the end.

I couldn't imagine where it came from.

Today I decided to visit Tony at the shoe store where he works.

It's in a mall, and nobody was in the store when I came.

"That's the best thing about working here," Tony said, "no customers."

He also said, "I gotta get outta here, man. This place is killin' me."

I was making copies with Julie today.

We put the finished copies into crates, and Julie carried them into the back, by the loading dock.

Every time she lifted one or put one down, she grunted and groaned.

She asked how many boxes we had left to fill and I said eight, and she made a really long steady groan.

I washed some clothes today.

While I was in the laundry room I noticed a shirt on the floor

It looked like it was a perfectly good shirt.

But it was full of dirt and lint and was discarded in a corner behind a trash can.

I saw Tony today. He said somebody called him for a job interview.

"I sent out fifty résumés last month," he said, "It's about time somebody called."

He said the call was from a shoe store on the other end of town.

"This is great!" he said. "Working there would be a million times better than working at my brother's shoe store."

Tony had his interview at the other shoe store today.

I asked him how it went and he said, "It went fine."

But by the way he said it, it didn't sound like it went fine.

Today I saw a guy picking coins out of the snow by a parking meter.

"I need to rethink my whole life—everything," Tony said today.

He said he realized that moving from one shoe store to another wasn't the way to get ahead.

He said, "It took me a long time to realize this."

I asked him what his big plans were and he said he didn't know.

Today Ruth came over and showed me the new coat she got.

It had a special kind of soft lining on the inside.

She said it was on sale and she couldn't pass it up.

She hung it on a chair and Mr. Peterson tried to climb up inside it.

I just sat around today and didn't do much of any- thing.

It was kind of rainy outside.

I thought of taking a nap, but I wasn't very tired.

So I just sat around and didn't do much of anything.

I was walking home today when I noticed some- body waiting at a bus stop.

She said, "Say, do you know when the B bus is supposed to get here?"

I told her I didn't know.

"It's late," she said. "It should've been here by now— I'm sure of it."

I didn't have to work at the copy store today so I slept in.

I woke up a few times, but never felt like getting out of bed.

After a while I realized I was sleeping even when I didn't feel like sleeping any more.

when I finally got up, it was 1:30.

Today I saw a guy in an old army coat walk into an ice cream store.

ice cream

He was unshaven and looked like he was shaking out of nervousness or something.

ice cream

I thought for a moment about the possibility that he would go in the store and shoot everybody.

But I figured the chance of that happening was pretty slim.

I was just sitting around today when Mr. Peterson came up and sat on my lap.

I scratched her back and she purred.

She looked at me and closed her eyes then opened them, like a slow-motion blink.

Then she got comfortable and fell asleep.

Today I saw Tony and he asked how it was going.

I said it was going fine.

He said he'd be quitting his shoe-store job any day now, "then look out, world!" he said.

I went home and ate a bowl of soup.

I went to the bookstore today to find a book to read.

I couldn't find anything that I felt like reading.

while I was walking home I noticed a torn piece of newspaper on the sidewalk.

I stood there for a while and read it.

I got some tacos for lunch today.

Dan came with me.

As we sat down, we noticed that we both ordered two soft tacos and a coke.

Dan commented on how most of the people in line seemed to prefer soft tacos to the hard-shelled kind.

Today at the copy store Hal came up to me and said, "Hey, Jim, how's it goin'?"

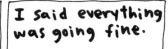

I said everything was going fine.

He stood there for a while, kind of looking around.

Then he swept some eraser shavings off the counter top with his hand.

While I was taking a shower today the soap slipped out of my hands and flew onto the floor.

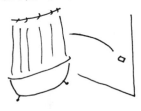

Mr. Peterson heard it fall and came over to smell it.

I looked at her, wondering if maybe she would bat it over to me.

And she ran away from it really fast.

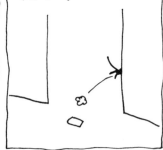

Today at the copy store Hal tuned the radio to a different station than usual.

But nobody else liked the station.

"Come on—this music is just fine," Hal said. "Now get back to work."

They kept bugging him, so he finally changed it back, saying, "Alright, alright, you whiners."

Today Tony told me he was going to be a millionaire in ten years.

"It's all right here in this awesome book," he said.

He showed me the part of the book that explained how to save and get interest so you can make a million dollars.

step 1
step 2
step 3

"This guy's a genius, Jim," he said. "This can't fail."

Today Hal called the newspaper to place a want ad for somebody to work weekdays.

When he hung up he said, "Jim, if you know anybody, tell 'em to apply."

When I got home I sat down with a plate of cookies to watch TV.

There was a show on that was predicting what life would be like in the next century.

I was sitting around today when Mr. Peterson started rubbing against me.

I scratched her head for a while and she purred like crazy.

Suddenly she popped her head up and stopped purring, as if she'd heard something in the other room.

She ran into the other room as fast as she could.

At the copy store today I worked with Julie.

I worked the cash register for all the self-service customers that came in.

Julie was making a bunch of copies of something that was due the next day.

When I heard the machine stop, I looked at Julie and she looked like she was asleep.

Steve came over today.

Mr. Peterson looked up at him and meowed a big bellowing meow when he came in.

meow

Steve said "Yeah, life is hard, isn't it? I know."

Mr. Peterson meowed again.

meow

Today Tony told me he needed to find another part-time job.

"If I'm gonna use this millionaire strategy, I need to put away a little bit more every month," he said.

I thought of telling him about Hal's copy store job, but figured he wouldn't be interested.

"I'm gonna look into something in radio or TV," he said.

I was talking with Dan a little bit today.

He told me he had once considered a career in the sciences.

"Science is like math," he said, "it's black and white—no gray areas.

And that's why he likes science, he said.

Today I watched TV for a while.

Then I went for a walk.

When I came back home and hung up my coat, the coat hook came out of the wall.

Around the inside edges of the little hole I could see tiny bits of plaster and wood.

Today I got off work at the copy store at 5:30.

While I was walking, a snowball suddenly hit me in the back of the head.

Then I heard somebody laughing, so I turned around to look at her.

"Gotchya!" she said.

Today I went to a craft & hobby shop with Ruth.

(She had to buy some felt.)

She picked out the felt she wanted and went up to the cashier.

I waited in line with her and looked at the ceramic lawn gnomes.

I washed a load of laundry today.

After taking the clothes out of the dryer, I brought them up to my apartment.

I was going to put them away, but Mr. Peterson jumped in the basket and got comfortable.

So I decided to put them away later.

Today Ruth showed me the thing she made with the felt she bought.

It was a sign that she made for her friend Janet.

It said, "A true friend is the greatest gift of all."

She explained how she glued the felt, some sparklers, and other things all together.

Today I was just sitting at my table, feeling kind of tired and bored.

I rested my head on my arms and started to doze.

Then Mr. Peterson jumped on the table. I could hear her purring.

Then she walked up onto my back and just sat there.

Today Steve rented a movie and he invited me over to watch it.

It was "Ben Hur."

It was about 3 hours long, and we watched the whole thing.

When it was over, Steve said. "I thought it would be retro-funny, but it was actually good."

Today Tony said "Hey— I'm going to Santa Monica for my brother's friend's wedding... wanna come?"

I said I would.

"Cool," he said. Then he told me all about the places we could go and things we could see.

"Oh— I should tell you," he said, "we leave tomorrow at 8 a.m."

Today Tony, his brother Mike and I got into Mike's car and headed for Santa Monica, CA.

Tony and Mike ate Doritos and talked a lot about the shoe store where they work.

The smell of vinyl seats started to make me feel a little carsick.

Tony turned to me and said, "Plenty of Doritos, Jim— dig in!"

We've been taking turns sleeping and driving in shifts.

Today, for a while, Tony was sleeping in the back seat and I was sitting in front with his brother Mike.

Even though I don't know Mike at all, we managed to have a conversation by talking about Tony.

when we ran out of things to say about Tony, we didn't say anything.

We arrived in Santa Monica last night.

Today Mike went off with his friend, and Tony and I went driving around the city.

Tony said, "Can you believe we're in sunny Californ-I-A? And on shoe store money!"

We tried driving up to the Hollywood sign, but we couldn't find the road up to it.

Today Tony and I went to Disneyland.

We waited in line for a long time for all the rides.

"The problem is, too many damned idiots come to this place!" Tony said.

We liked the Magic Mountain and Star Tours rides the best.

Today was Mike's friend's wedding, and Tony and Mike both went.	I sat around his house, where we were staying, and watched TV.	Then I went to the beach, which is only a few blocks from his house.	I listened to the ocean and watched all the people walking around.

We left Santa Monica today.	Nobody was saying much, and I got the impression Mike hadn't had a good time.	When Tony started to say something about it, Mike interrupted, saying "Shut up, Tony, I don't wanna hear it."	We drove all night and into the next day, in shifts.

When I walked up to my apartment today, Steve was just coming out of it.

(He took care of Mr. Peterson while I was gone.)

"Hey, Jim!" he said. "How was your big trip?"

I said it was pretty good.

I bought a Newsweek magazine today so I'd have something to read.

while I was walking home, I walked behind two people who were talking about their friends.

"I don't really have just, like, one best friend," one of them said.

"But I have, like, a bunch of really close friends, y'know?" she said.

Today I called to get a pizza delivered, with extra sauce, cheese and mushrooms.

The guy who delivered it was wearing a hat with the pizza company's logo on it.

I sat down and ate my pizza and read my Newsweek magazine.

I thought maybe they forgot to put the extra sauce on my pizza, but I couldn't really tell.

I worked at the copy store today.

Afterwards, I walked home the long way, by the lake.

There were people walking around the lake, and ducks sitting on the shore.

I decided to sit and watch people go by, and listen to the ducks.

Steve came over today.

"Hey, Mr. P," he said when he saw Mr. Peterson.

Then he said, "Jim, look what I brought."

It was the board game, Sorry.

We played a few games of Sorry, and Mr. Peterson kept pouncing on the game pieces.

Today Hal and I closed up the copy store at midnight.

When we were almost done, Hal said, "You can go home, Jim, I'll take care of the rest."

As I was walking away, I saw Hal through the window, wiping off the counters.

For a few seconds he concentrated his scrubbing in one little area, probably where there was a stain or something.

I was looking out my window today.

I saw a whole bunch of cars go by.

And some people.

Then Mr. Peterson jumped right in front of my face and I couldn't see anything.

Today Tony asked me if I wanted to play pool with him.

I said I would, and we walked over to the pool hall.

"I haven't played in a few weeks," Tony said, "But I still got the touch."

Then he hit the cue ball so hard it flew off the table.

Steve bought a new computer today.

"My old one was too slow on word processing," he said.

I watched him take it out of the styrofoam packaging and plug it in.

Once he had it hooked up, he played some sort of spaceship attack game.

I went over to Steve's place today to play on his new computer.

We decided to play Steve's favorite game, the one where you shoot spaceships.

Afterwords, we started talking about video games we used to play.

"There's no more good video games," steve said. "They're all 'waste the drug dealer' now."

I was riding the bus today with Steve.

We were looking at some of the poster ads above the windows.

One was for a chiropractor who had a free consultation offer.

free Consultation

chiropractor

Steve said, "It's free, Jim. We should go," and I said okay.

I went to the chiropractor today because they had a free consultation offer.

chiro-practor's office

The chiropractor asked me if I had back pain and I said not really.

"Good," he said. "It's never too early to start prevention."

And he showed me some exercises I could do so I would never have back pain.

I was hanging around with Tony today.	We got to talking about Steve and I mentioned that he just got a new computer.	"A computer?" Tony said, "How can he afford a computer when I can't even afford macaroni & cheese?"	I told him I guessed his parents gave him the money and he said, "I thought as much."

Today Tony said, "Hey, I got a great idea for a practical joke!"	He acted kind of secretive even though nobody was around who could have overheard us.	He said he figured out how to fool Steve into sending his computer away— by mailing him a fake recall notice.	He said, "This'll be the greatest hoax since my friend Dean threw water on me that one time."

Today I was watching TV with Ruth.

The channel wasn't coming in very well.

Ruth moved the antenna around.

"That's a little better, isn't it?" she said, even though it was just as bad.

Today Steve said, "Somebody's out to get me, Jim."

He showed me a letter he got in the mail today—a recall notice for his computer.

"When I called the company, they didn't know anything about it," he said.

"Also," he said, "the postmark is local, there's no model number, and some words are misspelled."

Today Tony chuckled and said, "I bet Steve's packing up his computer right this second.

I told him Steve got Tony's fake recall letter and knew right away that it was a fake.

"No way!" Tony said. "My plan was infallible!"

Then he shrugged and said, "Oh well, it's Steve's loss. It could've been a <u>classic</u> prank."

Today Steve and I ran into Tony.

Steve asked Tony, "You wouldn't happen to know anything about a fake recall notice for my computer?"

Tony said, "Aw, you're no fun. That could've been a great prank.

Steve listed all the reasons it didn't work, and Tony got tired of listening.

Today I heard some loud banging noises out in the hall.

It was construction workers, doing some repairs on the apartment building.

(They were tearing out a wall and putting in a new one, it looked like)

Mr. Peterson was scared to get close to the door because of all the noise.

Today I woke up to the sound of hammering and wood planks banging around.

Mr. Peterson was at the foot of the bed, trying to sleep, but with her ears angled back.

Later, while I was brushing my teeth, I noticed the mirror shaking from all the pounding.

when I touched it, it made me vibrate, too.

Today the sound of a power saw woke me up.

I could also hear the workers in the hall laughing and talking.

I opened my door to look at them and they didn't notice me at all.

I fed Mr. Peterson and watched her bob her head while she ate.

Today I was eating some graham crackers when I heard the door buzzer.

It was the UPS person, who asked if I'd accept a package for somebody next door.

I said I'd accept it, and signed his clipboard.

Later, I took the package to the person next door and he said, "All right! I've been waiting for this."

Today Steve was saying he wished they'd make an Aquaman movie.

"He's my favorite super hero, and they haven't made a movie of him yet," he said.

He asked me if I'd go to an Aquaman movie and I said I suppose I would.

"See—," he said, "they should make one!"

I ran into Tony today and we ended up going to the post office together.

We stood in line and Tony was looking at the FBI posters of wanted fugitives.

He pointed to one and said, "Hey, this one looks like you, Jim."

Then he yelled to the postal workers, "I found one! I'll hold him down, you call the cops!" and laughed.

I worked with Dan at the copy store today.

He was copying somebody's term paper or something.

He showed me a spelling error he found on it and asked me if he should fix it.

I said I didn't know what he should do.

I had lunch with Dan today.

We ate in the back of the copy shop.

Dan ate an egg salad sandwich he brought to work with him.

I ate a piece of pizza I got from the pizza place down the street.

Today at the copy store Julie and I were just sitting around.	It was a really slow day at the copy store.	Julie sighed and said, "Did you see the game Saturday?"	I didn't know what game she was talking about.

Today Steve got a survey in the mail.	It was from some kind of marketing place and had a lot of questions on it.	They wanted to know what kind of person Steve was and what he liked to buy.	Steve asked if I'd help him come up with silly answers for it some time.

I ran into Steve today.	He said he tried calling me last night but I didn't answer.	I couldn't understand, because I never heard my phone ring last night.	Steve said, "I figured you weren't home so I completely burglarized your place," he said, then chuckled.

Today Steve, Dan and I filled out the marketing survey Steve got in the mail.	Under race and religion and political opinion, Steve wanted to say he was an anarchist Catholic Eskimo.	Dan thought he should be a New Age Republican from Iraq.	He and Dan laughed and laughed, and couldn't decide which combination would be more fun.

Steve, Dan and I wrote more silly answers on Steve's marketing survey today.

Dan kept saying, "Tell 'em you make $5 a year—tell 'em $5 a year."

Steve didn't want to, but Dan kept insisting on it, so Steve finally wrote it down.

He also wrote that he has purchased 83 toasters in the last three months.

Steve mailed his marketing survey today.

He said, "I can't wait to see what kind of response I get."

He said he thought maybe he'd get some free coupons or something.

Afterwards, we played the space attack game on his computer and he beat me pretty bad.

Today I went to a movie with Ruth and Steve.

It was a midnight showing of "Pink Floyd the Wall."

When it was over, Ruth said, "I didn't get it."

Steve tried to explain it to her, then realized he didn't get it either.

Last night Mr. Peterson was standing on my back, kneading me with her paws.

I was trying to fall asleep, but she was too distracting.

Finally she sat at my feet and fell asleep.

I must have, too, because that's the last thing I remember.

Today I was adding something up on my calculator.

I could barely see the numbers on the display.

So I held it under the light and the numbers showed up perfectly.

(I guess my calculator is the solar-powered kind.)

Today I went to the store to buy a loaf of bread.

I couldn't find the kind I normally get, so I got a different kind.

I took it home and ate some, and it was pretty good.

I decided to get this new kind from now on.

Today I ate lunch with Dan in the stock room.

I noticed he brought some cookies with him that were jet black.

I asked him why he was eating burnt cookies.

He said, "I like things burnt... carbon adds flavor."

I found a balloon today, just lying by the sidewalk.

So I picked it up and took it home.

Mr. Peterson liked playing with the string on it.

She liked wrestling with the balloon too, and ran away in fear when it popped.

I was really tired today and felt like sleeping in.

But I had to get up to work at the copy store.

When I got there, I told Joel I'd felt like sleeping in.

He told me the same thing happened to him today.

At the copy store today I worked with Julie.

She had to re-arrange the little office supplies rack.

I pointed out that she missed a roll of tape that was still out of order, and she threw it at me.

But she wasn't really angry, she was just playing around, I'm pretty sure.

Today I noticed Mr. Peterson flipping from side to side on the floor.

She looked at me, then flipped around some more.

I figured she was bored, so I tickled her belly and she grabbed my arm and play-bit it.

I rolled her around and she grabbed me and bit me some more.

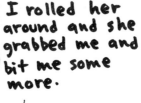

Today Dan was talking about apes, comparing them to humans.

He was talking about their social structure and behavior.

"Human society is very similar," he said, "There's male hierarchy, posturing, everyone knows their place.

Then Hal came out of the back room and told us all to get back to work.

I was trying to write something down today, but my pen was out of ink.

I looked around for another pen, but couldn't find one.

I couldn't find a pencil or anything else either.

So I just wrote with the bad pen, hoping it would indent the paper enough to be readable.

There was some kind of storm or something today.

The sky was green and it was raining really hard and the wind was banging on the window.

Mr. Peterson was hiding under the big chair.

Then Steve knocked on the door, soaking wet, saying, "Nice day, huh?"

Today during my lunch break at the copy store, I got a taco.

I was going to eat it in the back room of the copy store, but the weather was nice, so I sat outside.

Then Dan came outside with his bagged lunch and ate with me.

He asked what I was eating, looked closely at it, and said, "oh, a taco."

I went over to Steve's place today.

He rented "48 Hours" and we watched it.

When it was over, I stayed there and we talked about this and that.

He talked about philosophical things and Steve said, "I don't think life is absurd or meaningless. I think it's funny."

Today Ruth and I sat and tossed popcorn to the ducks. 	Ruth was telling me she liked the water. 	"I've always liked lakes, boat rides, and all that," she said." 	But she said it's been a long time since she's been on a boat, and she tried to recall when the last time was. 
I was watching TV today. 	There was nothing very interesting on, so I flipped around the channels. 	At one point I saw the same coffee commercial on two different channels at once. 	I eventually settled into an episode of "Gilligan's Island" that was pretty good. 

Today at the copy store I ate lunch with Dan in the back room.

He was eating a sandwich he brought from home.

As he was taking a bite, the sandwich slipped out of his hands and landed on the floor.

He looked down at it and said "I wish that hadn't happened."

Today I worked at the copy store almost 9 hours.

Joel was there and said he worked 9 hours today, too.

Julie told us she remembered working 12 hours straight once.

Then Hal said, "None of you have to take this job home with you— I do, and it's like working 24 hours a day."

"I did it, Jim," Tony said today. "I finally quit the shoe store."

"My brother thinks he fired me, but really I quit," he said.

I asked him what he was going to do now.

He said he didn't know, but that there was a whole world out there.

Today I got a letter from my mom.

She told me all about things she's doing and people I haven't seen in a long time.

And she said one of her first piano students was giving a really important recital.

I thought of a lot of things I could write back and say, but when I sat down to write, I couldn't think of anything.

Today Ruth came over and we ate some Cracker Jacks that she brought.

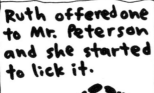

Ruth offered one to Mr. Peterson and she started to lick it.

Ruth laughed.

I told Ruth that Mr. Peterson likes to eat funny things sometimes.

Today Tony showed me his drivers license, which he had just gotten renewed.

"Don't I look like a dork?" he said, laughing.

He wanted to see my license, so I showed it to him.

"ooh, you do not photograph well, Jim," he said.

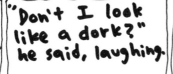

| Today I played some classical music on the radio.  | Mr. Peterson slept on top of one of the speakers, like she sometimes does.  | I was going to wash a load of clothes today.  | But all the washing machines were being used.  |

| Today I was just sitting around when I realized I was really tired.  | So I took a nap.  |  | I got up when Mr. Peterson knocked something off the table in the other room.  |

Today while I was watching TV, Mr. Peterson sat on my lap and purred.

I was watching some kind of loud car chase show, and the volume was turned way up.

But Mr. Peterson slept and purred despite all the noise.

Then, at one point, Mr. Peterson got up and shifted her position a little bit, then fell back to sleep.

Steve asked me to come to a baseball game today.

Steve isn't really a baseball fan or anything, but we decided it would be fun.

We sat and talked during the slow parts of the game.

Once, people started booing and Steve yelled. "Ya bum!"

I went out into the woods today.	I hiked around and looked at trees and stuff.	I tried to veer off the path once in a while, but the underbrush was too thick.	When I got home I plucked burrs and other things from my shoes.

I went to the store with Steve today to buy a candy bar.	The cashier said it was 53 cents, and I only had 50.	So she reached into her little penny box to get 3 pennies.	As we were leaving, Steve said, "They should have little boxes with $100 bills in them," and chuckled.

Today I was thinking of driving really fast.

It was like one of those video games where you drive a car.

I kept going faster and faster, screeching around curves and oil slicks.

I wanted to keep going, but my imagination kept crashing the car.

I was feeling kind of bored today.

So I went to a cafe and ordered a chocolate sundae.

The woman who took my order seemed like she'd rather be doing something else.

When I was done eating the sundae I felt kind of sick.

Steve made a casserole today and invited Ruth and me over to eat it.

He said he was worried it might be too spicy and asked what we thought.

I said it maybe was too spicy and Ruth didn't say anything.

Steve kept saying "c'mon, Ruth, be honest," until she finally said, "It's a bit spicy but it's good."

I went over to Tony's place today.

He was trying to swat a fly, and said he'd been stalking it for 10 minutes.

Finally it landed on a wall, and Tony moved slowly toward it.

He swatted it as hard as he could, and said, "once again, man conquers beast!"

smat!

I was reorganizing some books on my bookshelf today.	I made stacks on the floor and tried to put books on the shelf in some kind of order.	Mr. Peterson was sitting on the tallest stack, watching me.	It took me a long time because I kept stopping to read things.

Today I was over at Steve's place.	He showed me some 3-D glasses he still had from when he saw a 3-D movie a long time ago.	"I like 'em," he said. "Sometimes I wish I could just wear them like sunglasses."	But he said he wouldn't do that because people would think he was really weird.
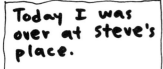			

Tony came by today to borrow some paper.

He said, "Hey, cat, how's it goin'?" when he saw Mr. Peterson.

I went into the other room to get some paper.

When I came out, I saw Tony having a moment with Mr. Peterson.

I sat at my desk today and did some word-find puzzles.

It was pretty dull, but I didn't have anything else better to do.

When I was little and did word-find puzzles, I always imagined the letters as giant towers.

And I had to find words by running around the edges of the letters to find the words.

I was a little late for work at the copy store today.

When I punched in, Hal said, "Running a little late, there, Jim?"

(He was flipping through account slips)

I told him I forgot I had to work until the last minute.

He forced a smile and kept flipping through the slips.

Today the sun was out, so Tony was sitting outside.

He said, "Hey, Jim, could you do me a favor? I forgot my sunblock—here's my key."

I went into Tony's room and found his sunblock in the bathroom.

I brought it out to him and he smiled at me and said, "Now if only I had some girl to rub it on for me."

Today I threw a crumpled-up piece of paper into the trash, but it missed.	I was pretty close to the garbage can, and couldn't believe I missed.	I picked up the paper, tried a second time, and missed again.	I finally made it on the third try.

I was making copies all day today.	Joel kept bringing me more things to copy.	He asked me if I was sick of making copies yet, and I said almost.	He paused, then said, "Jim, that was the worst attempt at humor I've ever heard."

Today Tony and I played darts at one of his hangouts.

He complained about the plastic ribbed dart board because the darts didn't always stick in it.

Then he hit the bulls-eye with a dart, but it bounced right off. "That was in!" he said. "That was in!"

Then he asked if he could have the points for it anyway.

I made a big sandwich today and sat and read the newspaper while I ate.

Mr. Peterson jumped up on the table and walked across the newspaper, so I set her back on the floor.

She ran into the other room and I kept reading and eating.

Then she started meowing at the top of her voice and wouldn't stop.

meow –
meow

Today Tony and I were walking around.

We came to a busy street and before I could react, Tony had run across.

He stood on the other side and waited for the rest of the cars to go by.

Then I crossed and we continued walking.

I bought a Popsicle today.

It really hit the spot.

When I was done eating it, I put the Popsicle stick in the trash.

And my fingers were all sticky.

Today Ruth called and said, "Hey, wanna do something?"

I asked her what she had in mind and she said, "How about a movie?"

We got together and looked in the paper and couldn't find any movies.

So we went to a play.

It was pretty good.

Today I scraped my hand on the corner of the window sill by accident.

It hurt pretty bad even though there was almost no mark.

I stared at my hand to see if I could see the microscopic throbbing.

I couldn't.

I decided to go over to Steve's house today.	When I got there I rang the buzzer but he didn't come to the door.	As I was leaving I saw Steve up in a tree, and he said, "Hi, Jim."	He told me he decided to climb a tree today because it would be fun. 
Today I marked my calendar for some important thing or other.	But my pen ran out of ink because it was pointing upward.	I tried to angle the pen down so the ink would flow better.	But, doing that, my writing was so sloppy I could barely read it.

I was walking down the street today when I saw a mailman delivering mail.

He had huge stacks of mail in his truck and a big bundle in his hands.

I thought of how hard it'd be to keep track of all that mail all over the world.

And I just couldn't imagine how they do it.

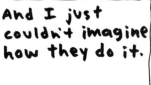

I went out to eat with Steve and Tony today.

We all decided it would be kind of fun to get together.

Steve told us about a crazy cable TV ad he was watching the other day.

Tony was saying he's up for a really good tele-marketing job.

Last night I got up at 3am. or so with an important idea in my head.

I turned on the light by my desk and it practically blinded me.

I wrote down the idea on a little piece of scrap paper.

When I got up this morning and read it, I couldn't figure out what I'd thought was so important about it.

Today as I was leaving my apartment, Mr. Peterson trotted back and forth by the door.

In the hallway I noticed a roof access panel.

I climbed the little ladder up to it to see if it would open.

But it was painted shut.

Today Dan and I got off work at the same time.

We walked towards his place, which is on the way to mine.

He told me that he hopes time travel can be possible someday.

I asked him why and he said, "Just because it would be neat, don't you think?

Ruth brought me a present today.

It was a rustic-looking wooden laundry basket she got at the mall.

She got it because she's seen how the handles on my old plastic laundry basket are falling apart.

Mr. Peterson attacked the new basket and started biting off pieces of it.

Today Julie was telling me that she was looking for a better job than the copy store.

"I have a college degree," she said. "I shouldn't be doing this."

Then Hal gave us a whole bunch of copies to make.

Julie looked at what Hal gave us, almost as if to evaluate whether it was worth being copied.

Today I saw Julie at the copy store

She wasn't working, so she didn't have her smock on.

She was making copies of her résumé so she could get a better job.

She looked closely at the copies to make sure they were perfect.

Today Mr. Peterson got a leaf somehow.	It must have come through the window when I had it open or something.	She was flipping over it and pouncing on it.	Then she carried it in her mouth and set it down in front of me.

I ran into Tony today.	He turned off his Walkman and said, "Hey, Jim, what's up?"	I said, "Not much."	Then a guy on a unicycle went by and Tony said, "Get a loada that guy!"

I watched TV all last night. 	There were a bunch of talk shows on. 	Today when I got up I felt a lot more tired than usual. 	I went to the corner store to get a newspaper and everybody seemed to be bustling. 
I worked at the copy store from noon till 8 today 	When I got home I was really hungry. 	I looked in the fridge to see if I had the makings of a sandwich. 	Luckily, I found just the things I needed. 

I went to the bookstore today and looked at the magazine rack.

I thought maybe I'd get a short story magazine or something.

I looked at the section with hot rod and wrestling magazines, too, just for fun.

A man walked in front of me and said, "Excuse me," and I stepped aside so he could get by.

I worked at the copy store today.

Hal came up behind me and watched me make copies.

I wondered if maybe I was doing something wrong.

Today I just sat and watched TV.

Steve came over for a while.

But then he left.

I don't think I realized he was there until after he left.

Today one of my kitchen drawers accidentally fell apart.

Mr. Peterson tried to eat the little bits of wood and cork that came off of it.

I nailed it back together and slid it back into place.

It works as good as new now.

Today I mailed a letter.

After I put it in, I opened the mailbox again.

My letter wasn't stuck to the side or anything, so I assumed it went in.

While the door was open, I decided to read when the collection times were.

Today I saw somebody who said he lost the little latch from his watch.

I helped him look for it.

"Found it!" he said, after a while.

Today I was throwing a crumpled-up piece of paper to Mr. Peterson.

She chased after it and pounced on it.

After a while she started batting it around herself, and I didn't need to throw it.

Then Ruth called and I described to her what Mr. Peterson was doing.

Today I went to a park.

I just sat on a bench.

Some people behind me were having a barbeque and I could smell the smoke from their grill.

Then two people on the path in front of me walked by saying, "mm—smells good!"

I was lying on my bed today, relaxing.

I was having trouble breathing because I was lying flat on my nose.

I didn't want to move my head though, because I was comfortable.

But eventually I had to move so that I could breathe.

Today I saw Tony shooting some baskets at the court near our building.

"I'm playing HORSE," he said. "Wanna play?" and I said sure, okay.

He said "Think fast!" and threw the ball at me.

I ducked to avoid being hit and it bounced into the street.

Today I was sitting at my desk when my light suddenly flickered off, then on again, with a soft clicking sound.

Mr. Peterson, who was sleeping at the foot of the bed, noticed it too, because she lifted her head up.

It didn't happen again, so I never figured out what caused it.

Mr. Peterson rested her head back on her hands.

Today I was sitting on my bed, staring at the ceiling.

I saw a tiny black dot that I thought, for a second, was moving.

Then I saw Mr. Peterson looking intently at the same spot, making a chirping sound like a half-meow.

I decided the spot must be some sort of bug or something.

Today at the copy store it was really busy.

We had copying jobs stacked up on the counter and long lines of customers.

I gave somebody her copies and she said, "Wait, these aren't mine."

I looked through the stack until she pointed and said, "That's mine—the one right there."

Today I was washing my dishes after eating a sandwich.

A little drop of water flung right onto Mr. Peterson's head, and she shook her head and ran away.

When I finished the dishes I sat down and turned on the radio.

The speakers just popped really loudly—even with the volume all the way down.

Today Hal called me into his office and said, "Jim, you've been here almost two years, haven't you?"

I said I wasn't quite sure (I was looking at the pictures of his family on his desk.)

"Anyway," he said, "I figure it's time you got a 25¢ per hour raise."

After a few seconds he said, "Haven't you got any response to that, Jim?"

I was hanging around with Steve today.

I mentioned that Hal gave me a 25¢ per hour raise at the copy store.

He said he didn't think that added up to much over a week.

He figured out exactly how much it came out to, and it wasn't very much at all.

Today I got up a little late and had to hurry to the copy store.

When I got there, Hal was putting in an alarm system.

The district manager of the copy store was there, too.

They were standing around watching the guy from the alarm place install the alarm.

I took my radio into the repair place today.

The woman at the shop asked me what was wrong with it and I said the speakers popped even with the volume turned all the way down.

She put a tag on it and told me they'd call when it was fixed.

(She had a little tuft of hair sticking straight out of her head that I couldn't help but notice.)

Today Dan said I should come over to his place to watch a movie some time.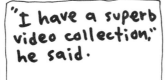

"I have a superb video collection," he said.

Joel, who was walking past us at the moment, chuckled to himself.

When Dan asked him what was so funny, Joel said it was nothing.

Today I went to Dan's place after work.

I couldn't believe how messy it was.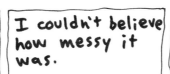

Dan said he had a really great video we could watch.

He said, "It's here somewhere," while sifting through clothes, garbage and stuff.

Today I was sitting down for a long time and my leg fell asleep.

I could barely make use of the leg, and walked around awkwardly.

Mr. Peterson looked at me with her eyes wide, like I was going to stomp on her.

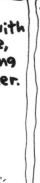

The feeling eventually went away and I was able to walk just fine.

Today I was getting something out of the cupboard when a can of beans fell on my head.

It hurt really bad, and I went to the mirror to see if there was a mark or anything.

I couldn't see anything.

But I felt like there was a bump as big as a corn cob sticking out of my head.

Today Ruth came over and we just sat and talked.

I mentioned that I got hit in the head by a can of beans yesterday.

She winced and said, "Ooh, that must have hurt."

I told her that it did.

Today Steve and I went over to Dan's place to watch "The Godfather."

Dan had a whole bunch of papers, clothes and stuff on the couch that he threw onto the floor so we could sit.

Steve and Dan talked about the movie while we watched it because they'd seen it before.

They pointed out their favorite parts and got excited during the shoot-out parts.

I was watching TV today.

Mr. Peterson was sitting on my lap.

I watched an episode of Star Trek that I'd seen before.

Then there was some kind of talk show on that I eventually lost interest in.

Today when I got to the copy store, Hal was talking to some police officers.

I went in back to punch in and found out from Julie that the copy store got robbed the night before.

"They stole some paper and messed up Hal's office," she said.

I looked at Hal and he was answering "no" and "not really" to a bunch of the officers' questions.

Today at the copy store, Hal was telling us what he thought of the copy store robbery.	"The police said it might've been a disgruntled former employee," he said, "but I doubt that."	Then Dan said, "They obviously tore up your office looking for money."	Then Joel looked at Dan and said, "Duh."

Ruth came over today.	We sat and ate popcorn and talked.	She was saying that she's always wanted to go to Europe.	"But I guess I wouldn't mind just learning one of the languages instead," she said.

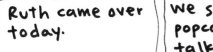

Today when I got up, I realized I'd had a dream about today.

I dreamt that I got up, went to work and everything else.

Nothing weird happened in the dream, but now I thought I'd already lived through the day.

So I felt like I was having to do it all over again.

Today I got up and fed Mr. Peterson, as usual.

I made myself a bowl of cereal and read the newspaper while eating.

I could hear Mr. Peterson chomping her food.

I worked at the copy store till 8:30 and nothing very eventful happened.

Today Steve came to the copy store and wanted me to make a copy for him.

(Hal was sorting the colored paper right behind me.)

When I gave Steve the copy, he asked, "So, you gonna give me this for free?"

Hal looked up and said, "You better not be giving out copies, Jim."

Today I was visiting Tony. (His apartment is on the top floor of the building.)

We looked out the emergency exit at the end of the hall.

Through the grate of the fire escape I could see the alley way, seven stories down.

Tony nudged me a little bit, yelling, "Watch out, Jim!" and it really startled me.

I made some brownies today.	I bought the brownie mix at the store the other day.	All I had to do was mix in an egg and some water, and bake them.	They tasted pretty good.

I got a free issue of Details magazine in the mail today.	They wanted me to subscribe, so they gave me an issue free.	I looked through it while I ate lunch (a left-over piece of pizza).	Mr. Peterson jumped on the table and sat right on top of the magazine.

Today Dan came over and we watched TV.

He looked through the TV schedule to see what was on.

We decided there was nothing interesting on, but we sat and watched it anyway.

The reception wasn't very good, so Dan adjusted the antennae every so often.

Tony came by today.

He told me he found a great job, "with five-fifty an hour plus commission!"

He said it was a telemarketing job.

He looked at the stuff on my table and said, "You get Details? No way!"

Today Ruth and I made some things out of paper maché.	Ruth mixed up a batch of it because she thought it would be fun.	She made a Viking helmet and I made a turtle.	Our hands got coated with the crusty goop.

I was throwing Mr. Peterson's ball around today when the phone rang.	It was somebody reading off a script, "Sir, don't you think cable TV is worth less than thirty cents a day?"	Then the person suddenly burst out laughing, and I recognized the voice as Tony.	"I thought I'd call and give you my spiel," he said. "Pretty good, huh?"
ring			

Today I was walking down the sidewalk when I slipped on some ice and fell.

People, standing on the other side of the street or wherever, stopped what they were doing and looked at me.

They didn't laugh or help or anything. They just looked.

I got up and continued walking.

Tony, Steve and I were hanging out today.

We were talking about which TV shows we liked, and Steve said The Simpsons.

"But I can't watch it at Jim's," he said, "because your reception is about as good as the moon's."

"Then Tony said to me, "Cable TV is only like thirty cents a day," which is from his phone sales pitch.

I was watching TV today and the channel wasn't coming in very well.	I adjusted the antennae but it didn't help.	I remembered Dan saying I should put some tin foil on the antennae, so I tried that.	The reception was a little better after that.

I was walking with Tony today on his way to work.	"Hey, you should come in and meet some of the clowns I work with," he said.	I followed him into a big office filled with people talking on phones, and he pointed to an old guy smoking and said, "This is chuck."	Then Tony announced, "Hey, everybody, this is my buddy Jim," and a few people looked but nobody seemed interested.

Today at the copy store Julie and I were making a bunch of copies. 	Our lunch break was just a few minutes away, but Julie said she wasn't hungry. 	She asked, "What should I do on my break?" 	I said I didn't know and she said, "Maybe I'll drop dead." 
I was sitting in my chair today when Mr. Peterson started attacking my feet. 	Then she looked at me, flipped over, then hid under the table. 	The phone rang, and Mr. Peterson darted into the other room. ring 	It was the audio repair place saying my radio was fixed. 

I went to the audio repair place today to pickup my radio.

While I was there, I asked if they sold antennae, because mine was broken.

The woman working there asked me to describe the problem, so I explained my bad TV reception.

She said, "why don't you have cable?" and I said I didn't know.

Today I called the cable TV company.

"I think you're the last guy on earth without cable," Steve said yesterday.

I told the person on the phone I wanted to sign up for cable TV.

She put me on hold and I took the opportunity to unravel my phone cord.

Today the cable TV guy came.	He had a big belt full of tools and hooked up my TV really fast.	"Mind if I use your phone?" he said. I said sure and he dailed his number.	While he was waiting for it to answer he pointed to Mr. Peterson and said, "Hey cat, how's it goin'?"

I let Mr. Peterson outside today.	She sniffed around by the stairs, like she usually does.	A dog walked by and stared at her and stretched his leash to the limit.	Mr. Peterson stared back, crouched down and froze solid.

Tony came over today. 	"Whad'ya say I watch your TV for a while?" he said. 

I said okay.

He plopped down on the couch and asked, "How's the cable TV workin' out for ya?"

I worked at the copy store till closing today.

After we locked up, Hal said, "See you tomorrow, Jim. Have a good one."

I walked home the long way, by the lake.

When I got home, I sat and listened to a talk show on the radio until I fell asleep.

Today Mr. Peterson and I saw the same dog we saw the other day.

This time he walked right up to Mr. Peterson.

She hissed at him and he walked away as if he wasn't interested anymore.

Mr. Peterson stayed in her cowering position for a few minutes after.

I rode the bus with Ruth today.

(She likes to take the bus sometimes instead of driving her car.)

We noticed that whenever another bus passed our bus, the two drivers always waved.

"I think that's nice," Ruth said.